# Acknowledgement

I am sitting here on a cloudy Sunday morning in September no longer wondering what it feels like to be an author because I have just completed my first book. Like many people, I've been thinking about writing a book for many years. This year, I simply said to myself "I'm going to make it happen" – and here I am, on my leadership journey, hitting a personal milestone.

They say that timing is everything, and the time feels right for me. It's not just about wanting to make my mark but I feel that over the years I have learnt much about how to lead with purpose, clarity, and making a positive impact. I feel I have become someone who is well grounded, faces the future with optimism, can adapt to opportunities, and embrace lifelong learning.

For this, I wish to acknowledge firstly my parents. In particular my late father, for sharing with me his general common sense approach to everything in life. My immediate family, both at home and those at work – my team at Pathway Group, thank you to you all. A big thank you to my business partners, we all have had dark moments as well as light ones, but we have stuck together for nearly 20 years now and I appreciate you burning the midnight oil alongside me.

To Barry Mapp, thank you for the wonderfully thoughtful foreword. To Adrian Kibbler from AKPR - your proof reading and critique was much needed feedback. Thank you for being a companion on this path. To the team at Digital Glue for working closely with me in designing and proofreading, best of luck with your new office and the next phase in your business journey.

I have been privileged to meet so many people on my journey through my career and each one of you has made an impact on me in one way or another. A particular mention goes to my team at Pathway2Grow who have been an inspiration to me.

Finally, to leaders of businesses, business owners, and potential business owners everywhere. I hope this book contributes in some way in giving you knowledge and inspiration to help you achieve any goal you set out to achieve.

# Canny Bites

### 52 bites of business wisdom for leaders and entrepreneurs

### Safaraz Ali

# Foreword

I found it interesting that Saf asked me to write a foreword to this book. I'm not sure if he was aware, but I actually have a general dislike for books that look like they might be a big list of random ideas - One Hundred ways/tips/ideas to improve your life/work/happiness/productivity, etc.

So on the face of it; this is a book I ought to dislike. However, not so! A few things in particular warmed me to this book. I love the layout and the graphics. I love the simplicity of the content and, perusing the index, I could immediately see that the book isn't just a list of 52 random business ideas. Instead the whole work is structured into meaningful, useful segments and this makes the book truly 'canny'. Not just canny in the sense that each individual 'bite' is relevant to budding entrepreneurs and leaders of organisations big and small, but canny in that - for me at least - the whole thing is well 'thought-through'. The thinking is all 'joined-up' and cleverly put together. The whole book makes sense.

The book also demonstrates Saf's position as a thought leader in the business space. Concepts like 'hiring staff should not be a tick box process', that 'solutions are often counter-intuitive', and 'business KPI's should be simple, few in number, and relevant' - all good stuff. I'd take this opportunity to add one thing - when using KPI's keep in mind that there will always be the unknown (what you don't know you don't know) - just one of the reasons why counter-intuitive solutions to problems often work. And as Lloyd Nelson, the statistician, reminded us - the most important figures needed for effective management are often unknown or unknowable (see Deming's Book 'Out of the Crisis') So, when monitoring KPI's, managers should know about measurement, natural variation, and that one can't interpret measures like KPI's effectively without some knowledge of statistical thinking (if we ignore the natural variation in our measurements, we react to every data point fluctuation as though it means something significant but far more often than not this is just 'noise' in the measuring system! Most fluctuations in measurements are attributable to 'common cause' and not 'special cause' variation).

Further important concepts for leaders and entrepreneurs are to be found in the sections on open mindset; knowing when not to take action; being the dumbest person in the room (beginner's mind), and acknowledging how emotions influence decisions.

Finally what makes Canny Bites such a 'must read' is that Safaraz has personal experience of all the concepts he outlines in the book. For example, on team building, he has helped build some great teams at the Pathway Group. On Networking, he has set up a successful Business Networking Group with Pathway2Grow. On branding, he has created the 'Coffee and Natter', 'Chutney and Chat' and other remarkable brands in the West Midlands business sphere. And on growing a business and goal-getting, his achievements speak for themselves.

Never stop learning, in your career or in your business. The world we live in is a world of lifelong learning. There are times in our life when we do not have all the answers or the drive, and so we need to look beyond ourselves. And that is why you should read this book. I highly recommend it.

**Barry Mapp**
*Thought Leader in Accelerated Learning and Brain and People Development, Mind Mapping & Learning Coach with 18,000 students worldwide*

# Preface

**Whether you're a business owner or a leader in an organisation, if growth is a primary objective of yours, an entrepreneur's mindset is crucial. But what makes up this mindset?**

To me, the central skill to the entrepreneurial mindset is emotional intelligence. When you can understand somebody else's perspective, problems, and frustrations, you are in the best position to build bridges and develop relationships. But being emotionally savvy means being in tune with yourself first, and being able to answer questions such as 'Where am I now?' and 'Where would I like to be?'. Without this understanding of your abilities, strengths, and weaknesses, it's unlikely you'll ever be in the position to understand others, motivate them, and help to drive growth in your organisation.

As such, the first rule of developing an entrepreneurial mindset is, whatever you do in your business or your role, it needs to be enjoyable, fruitful, and continually challenging. These things will encourage you in your personal growth, which will eventually translate to professional growth.

**So how can we achieve this personal growth?**

My late father used to tell me, "seek knowledge and wisdom, even as far as China". This is something that has stuck with me since. And it is that very notion of seeking, sharing, and retaining wisdom in which we can find the seeds of personal growth. Without the assistance, advice, and inspiration of others, the gears of our mind grind to a halt.

I'm a big fan of quotations - there's a lot of wisdom to be found in them. But there are some quotes that stay with us, and some that we forget almost immediately, or that don't stay with us longer than a week. I find that our memories are more attuned to stories. That's why the 'bites' contained within this book have been laid out in a carefully planned order. They are intended to take you through the steps of personal and professional growth. At the same time, however, each one in turn has its own treasure trove of wisdom to reveal.

Feel free to read what grabs your attention. This book should be fun to read as you see fit, whether that's from start to finish, or as a pick-and-mix-situation. There will be some bites that you just don't get and others you love and will never forget.

I sincerely hope that you will enjoy the format of the stories and embrace their lessons. The completed book, with its 52 bites, is much greater than the sum of its parts; it is designed to share with busy business people know-how, wisdom and advice and in a way that is more memorable, practical, and adaptable to you. However you choose to read it, I wish you the best on your journey.

**Safaraz Ali**

# Contents

## Chapter 1: Networking that works

## Chapter 2: Goal-setting and goal-getting

## Chapter 3: Better you, better business

## Chapter 4: Mastering decision making

## Chapter 5: Some lessons in leadership

## Chapter 6: Building a winning team

13

# Networking that works

Tips and tricks for a
well-connected business

1. Getting networking right

2. Pep up the pleasantries

3. Bravado is baloney

4. The secret to never missing an opportunity

5. Network for partnerships

6. Why size matters

7. The Law of Big Numbers

8. The power of mastermind groups

# 1. Getting networking right

While networking is seen as a crucial way to develop businesses, it doesn't come naturally to everybody. The art of networking is very precise; if you're quiet, you'll never make an impression on anybody, but if you're overzealous, you certainly will – just not necessarily the impression you wanted to make.

## So how can you make networking work for you?

The first step is about **balance**.

Good networking etiquette is about balance and finding a natural position between being assertive and being considerate. Networking works best if you're confident, but you must also take care not to overshadow everyone else.

The second step is about **listening**.

Good networking is based around good conversation, and good conversation is the keystone to a good relationship – whether personal or professional. We all know that the key to good conversation is about listening and responding in an interested and helpful manner. Don't use networking as an opportunity to sell, but an opportunity to learn more. Ask questions and respond in thoughtful ways to help build up a rapport.

The third step is about **building a relationship**.

Follow up with your new contacts and keep up to date with their business. Remaining in touch will help establish a relationship, and when that person faces a challenge, you will be better placed to discuss with them how you can help them.

*Chew on this:*
**Can you remember any networking faux-pas you've made? What did you learn from them?**

# 2. Pep up the pleasantries

Small talk is a key skill when it comes to networking - it's a crucial tool in establishing equality and familiarisation between two people who have just met.

Often, the temptation is to default to cliché conversations about traffic or the weather, but this is unlikely to help you make your mark. So how can you stand out from the crowd without being controversial?

## Start with substance

**"Nice weather, isn't it?"**

How many times have you opened with this line? It's easy to do, but it doesn't really mean anything or help you get to know the other person. Start with something of substance – talk to people about mutual connections, events you have been to, or training that you're undertaking that they might be interested in.

Ermmm...

## Add humour

Tickling someone's funny bone is a great way to be remembered. Add a little bit of humour now and again where you can, but remember to avoid controversial topics.

## Ask questions

This is key, but the secret is in how you do it. Don't be inquisitive, but exploratory. For example, add context to your questions. Rather than saying "what is your biggest challenge right now?" or "how can I help your business?", ask someone what their business is and how a recent event or relevant news piece is currently affecting their business, whether for better or for worse.

*Chew on this:*
**What small talk pitfalls do you tend to fall into, and how can you avoid them?**

# 3. Bravado is baloney

**"Never let them see you sweat!"**

**"Keep your weaknesses close to your chest!"**

**"Don't read like an open book!"**

Often, when it comes to networking, we're encouraged to present ourselves in a way that is strong and impressive in the hope that others will naturally gravitate towards us. There is, however, one undeniable problem with going into a networking event with this attitude: **it simply doesn't work.**

This attitude is not confidence - it is bravado. And Bravado is baloney.

Yes, presenting yourself with confidence is key when it comes to attracting individuals and business opportunities, but bravado – for example bragging, or seeking attention at all times - is likely to put people off, rather than help them warm to you. It suggests that you're insincere, have something to hide, or are overcompensating for something.

A certain level of vulnerability, on the other hand, is a good thing. In many ways, it is a strength, rather than a weakness. It shows that you're human. Being open with the people you meet, confiding in them and being authentically you, is a great way to build relationships on trust and mutual understanding. This way you're more likely to find yourself surrounded with open and honest people, rather than superficial people.

*Chew on this:*
## How can you create honest and authentic relationships with people you meet?

# 4. The secret to never missing an opportunity

### How many opportunities have you missed?

Most people consider themselves the kind of person who is ready to seize any opportunity, yet many of these same people actually miss out on opportunities that are directly in front of them without even realising it.

### Why?

Because they are closed.

This doesn't mean they actively turn down opportunities, but that they are simply too busy looking *elsewhere*. They're seeking specific people and specific companies. This means that they inadvertently dismiss others that could have been great opportunities, without even testing the water.

You can spot these people at networking events because they tend to say things such as,

**"I'm only looking to meet high net worth individuals"**

or

**"I'm here to connect with Decision Makers"**

'Closed' people don't realise that you can often be completely surprised by connections and opportunities that at first did not seem like much.

The reason they haven't realised this yet? They *simply haven't tried being open.*

## The secret to never missing an opportunity?

Be open and don't write anyone off – you just never know where things might lead.

*Chew on this:*
**How can you maintain an open mind when you're meeting new people?**

# 5. Network for partnerships

**Has teaming up with another business ever crossed your mind?**

You may think you're better off alone, but a strategic alliance with another business is a great way for a business to expand their reach. It's an opportunity for like-minded businesses to help each other by sharing ideas and recommending useful services.

A good example of this is the 'Wedding Mafia'. This is when planners, dress shops, florists, car hire businesses, venues, photographers, and caterers team up to work together. When one of them gets wedding business, they bring in the others, making it difficult for anyone outside of the "mafia" to get referrals.

So, what can your business gain from a strategic alliance?

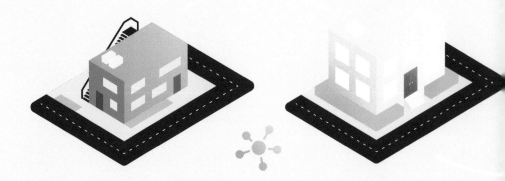

### Sharing resources and information

You may be in the same field, but you're likely to have expertise in different areas. Both businesses will grow stronger through sharing knowledge and learning from one another.

### Access to innovative and new technologies

Another business may introduce you to a tool that totally changes how your business functions. Without your alliance, you may never have discovered it and missed an opportunity to innovate.

### Reduced competition

Joining forces with a like-minded business means that not only will you immediately lose them as a direct competitor, but you will have a competitive advantage over other similar businesses through your pooled resources and skills.

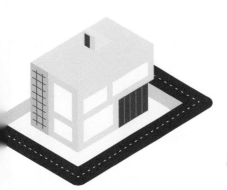

*Chew on this:*

**How could teaming up with another business improve your services or products?**

# 6. Why size matters

When it comes to your network, which is more important: quality or quantity?

Most people would instantly say **quality**, but what if I were to tell you that it's **quantity** you should care about?

According to social marketing expert Thomas Power and his Law of Big Numbers; quantity is what business owners should focus on. In his words, you have to **"pour stuff in to get stuff out"**

Think of quantity as an **input**, and quality as an **output**.

If your network is made up of **100** people, statistically, you will only do business with one of them.

If it is made up of **1,000** people, statistically,
you will only do **good** business with one of them.

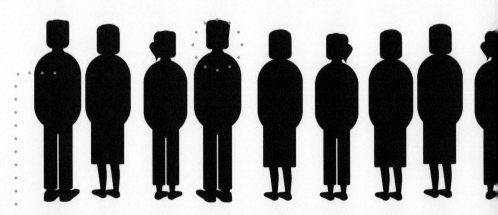

And if your network is made up of **10,000** people, statistically, you will only make a **mentor or true supporter** out of one of them.

Your network is a numbers game. The more you put in, the more likely you are to get high quality value out. Not everyone you meet will add value to your business - it's unlikely that you'll find a mentor and somebody who truly champions your brand in the first 100 people you meet.

Quantity increases your chances of quality - this is the power of having a big network.

*Chew on this:*
**How big is your network, and is it big enough to help you find more quality connections?**

# 7. The Law of Big Numbers

One of the benefits of having a high quantity of people in your network is that they can help you become a leading expert in your field.

**How? It's all about the quantity of input and the quality of your output.**

Having a large network simply means that you have access to more information. More people email you with links to interesting articles, more people tweet you their opinions, and more people involve you in discussion.

As your network increases, the quantity of input increases.

This gives you more knowledge.

As you expand your knowledge and become more informed, the quality of your output will increase, meaning you will be better placed to share good advice and counsel people on what is good practice.

If you have a lot of knowledge, more people will want to extract it from you. More people will invite you to events to speak, ask for your opinion on their problems, and put you in touch with other people for you to give them advice.

Essentially, they will be putting you and your business in front of people who need it.

*Chew on this:*
**How can you use your network to grow your reputation as an expert?**

# 8. The power of mastermind groups

## What is a mastermind group?
The term refers to a gathering of like-minded people who come together to brainstorm, educate, and support each other's business goals. Joining a mastermind group is something that many business leaders find beneficial.

## What can you gain from a mastermind group?
Every business has its ups and downs. Hearing about other people going through similar challenges to you can help you to learn. By joining a mastermind group, business leaders can support each other when things aren't going well, and congratulate each other when they are. Sharing experiences, both good and bad, will give you affirmation in what you are doing and why you are doing it.

### Different perspectives

Whether you agree or disagree, hearing new perspectives can help you find solutions you may not have found otherwise. Often, an outsider's perspective can be more insightful than a colleague's because they are considering something with a fresh outlook.

### Accountability

By sharing goals with others, you will be more likely to achieve them. This is because it is not only you holding yourself accountable. In sharing your goals, others will make it more likely you follow through with plans, and encourage you when you need support.

### Varying skillsets

Other people have skills, resources, and knowledge that you don't. Sharing in other people's knowledge and skills – and sharing yours in  return will mean that you have a pool of different resources to help achieve your goals.

*Chew on this:*
**How can your business benefit from the support and opinions of other business leaders?**

# Goal-setting and goal-getting

How to create your strategy
for success

HOLIDAY

# 9. Are you a goal-SETTER or a goal-GETTER?

If you've ever done any research into effective goal-setting, you may have heard about the now famous urban myth about the 1979 Harvard MBA Business school study.

The story goes that a group of researchers conducted a study on the Harvard Business School graduating class to assess the power and effectiveness of goal-setting. The graduates were asked one question; **have you set written goals and created a plan for their attainment?**

According to the story, ten years later, the 13% of the class that had written goals but had not created plans to achieve them were making **twice as much money** those who had made no plans at all.

**84%**
**Had no**
**goals at all**

**3%**
**had written down goals**
**and had created plans**
**to accomplish them.**

**13%**
**had goals written down,**
**but had made no plans**
**to achieve them.**

But even more impressive was the fact that the **3% that had both written goals and a plan were making ten times as much as the rest of the whole class.**

While this story may not be true, there's no denying that being clear about your goals is crucial in achieving them. In 2007, Professor Gail Matthews at the Dominican University of California did produce a study which proved that having clear goals, a plan, and a mechanism for holding yourself accountable makes you more likely to achieve them.

We all know that goal-setting is important, but there's a significant difference between setting goals, and setting yourself up to achieve them. To be a goal-getter, rather than simply a goal-setter, we must always ensure that we have in place the means to achieve them.

*Chew on this:*
**When was the last time you reflected on your goals, and have you written them down with a plan of action?**

*This could be setting smart, specific goals, or sharing your goals with an accountability partner – such as a mentor or even a mastermind group – to remind you to be committed to working towards your objectives.*

# 10. Why it's time to re-evaluate the reasons you started your business

Business Growth International compiled the results of studies from the likes of McKinsey and Harvard to get the top 5 reasons why people decided to start their own business. According to the report, these reasons were:

- **More freedom** – the ability to arrange work around your life, rather than the other way around
- **More time** – the flexibility to focus on the things that are most important to you
- **More money** – the chance to work hard and support the lifestyle that you desire
- **To serve the world and solve a problem** – having the ability to take action and give back to others
- **Less stress** – to have the freedom to worry less and enjoy life more

## Do any of these reasons sound familiar to you?

Take a moment to remember for what reasons you started your own business. How are they going for you? Sometimes, it can be all too easy to get caught up in the nitty gritty and ignore what it is that you are working towards.

If you feel like your original goal is a distant memory, it's worth spending time to re-evaluate your strategy and find out what you can do to

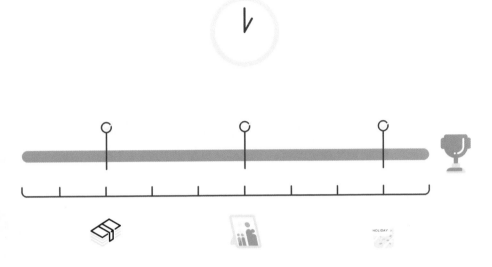

change that. While "having more money" is a common and legitimate goal to have, setting a specific and measurable goal is more likely to get you there. How much money do you want to make, and by when? If you want to have more free time, what time is it that you need? Do you want to spend the evenings with your family, or do you want the flexibility to book a round-the-world trip next year?

Having the right goals, a strong plan, and a good support network can help you to fulfil the objectives that made you take the leap. It's time to re-evaluate the reasons you started your business in order to make sure that you can really achieve them.

*Chew on this:*
**Re-evaluate the reasons you started your business. What do you need to do now in order to achieve them?**

# 11. Motivation is not the same as dedication

Most people usually fail to understand the difference between motivation and dedication. In business and in life, it is important to know the the difference between the two.

Someone might seem extremely motivated by something, but in reality lack the dedication to go out and do it.

For example, a student at university might dream of becoming a journalist and feel motivated when they picture themselves as one in the future. But they might fail to work hard to gain the experience needed in this competitive field because they don't make the time or because they're easily put off by a setback. In this case, the person is not dedicated enough to persist and battle against the adversity.

## Dedication is about being committed to the cause even when it's difficult

Motivation is emotional, and will come and go depending on a whole host of factors. No-one can expect to be highly motivated all of the time. Getting up at 4am for a 10k run when you feel great is **MOTIVATION** but getting up for a 10k run when it is cold and wet and you feel awful is **DEDICATION**.

Motivation is great, but dedication is better.

In business, you should surround yourself with people who are dedicated, as they will show you how to persevere when things go wrong - not just how to work hard off the back of a good streak.

*Chew on this:*
**How do you stay dedicated when the going gets tough? How can you use this to help inspire others to stay dedicated?**

39

# 12. Get real – and stay that way

Theodore Roosevelt, US President from 1901 to 1909, once said:

> **"Keep your eyes on the stars and your feet on the ground."**

In other words – ambitious plans are great, but it is important to keep in touch with reality.

Ego is the enemy of success – in all aspects of life. In Greek tragedy, Hubris is the quality of excessive pride, which often led the main character to believe they were capable of something they were not. More often than not, this personality trait led to the tragic downfall of those who possessed it.

In politics, delusions of grandeur can prove dangerous - as history has shown. For example, the former Prime Minister Tony Blair said that the worst part of the job was that it removed him from reality.

Similarly, in business, it is important to have regular reality checks. Without them, it becomes all too easy to get wrapped up in "the vision" and lose sight of how you will get there.

In order to be a strong and effective organisation, you must not surround yourself with 'yes men', but with people who are able to challenge you, ask difficult questions, and keep you grounded.

Be ambitious, but also understand that when reality goes out of the window, success will soon follow.

Chew on this:
**What can you do in order to always keep grounded?**

41

# 13. What's the difference between strategy and tactics?

Too many organisations do not understand the difference between strategy and tactics, and how they can help you achieve your objective.

Objectives set the destination, strategy explains how you will get there, and tactics provide the detail of each step.

A good objective, and even more importantly a good strategy, should be simple enough that it can be effectively communicated, understood, and ultimately achieve 'buy in' from those within the organisation.

For example, a business that offers networking might have the the **objective** of being the **networking organisation of choice** for small and medium sized businesses...

Their strategy might be to **build a sustainable national network** of vibrant and highly regarded groups...

Their tactics would be the details of **who runs the groups, where they are, how they are promoted, etc.**

Having a clear strategy means there is a framework against which to check if the tactics – the detail – really delivers and helps you to achieve your objectives.

*Chew on this:*

**Are your objectives, strategy, and tactics clearly defined and aligned with one another?**

# 14. The golden rules of developing a good strategy

Pep Guardiola, the successful former manager of FC Barcelona, was once asked what his objective for the team was. He replied: 'To try to win everything'. His strategy? 'Play better football than any other team.' As simple as it may seem, this strategy adheres to the golden rules of a good strategy. These are:

## Make the strategy simple

Guardiola's strategy is easy to understand. It is clear to see how this would help Barcelona to win more matches, and it was therefore easy for the team to buy into.

## Never mix strategies

The strategy was built upon one, strong idea. Doing this means that you only invest time and effort into one dependable thing.

## Never lose sight of the strategy

Success is built on improvement. In Barcelona's case, their training was aimed at improving so that they played better than any other team.

## Do not confuse strategy with tactics

Guardiola's strategy does not state how often or how hard the team were going to train. These are tactics. Instead, this strategy can be used to measure whether these tactics are working.

## A strategy needs to be consistently applied

There would be no point if FC Barcelona only tried to be the best team sometimes. Consistency is key when it comes to success as it will help you improve and grow.

A company without a strategy will try anything – as the saying goes, "If you don't know where you are going, any road will get you there". If you have a clearly defined ambition, you should know how you're going to get there. And if you do manage to get there by doing anything and everything, chances are you won't be able to do it again because you don't know what it was that was successful the first time.

*Chew on this:*
**Which of these rules do you always follow? Which do you rarely follow?**

# 15. The keys to success: choosing your KPIs

## What is a KPI?

KPI stands for key performance indicator. Businesses use KPIs to measure the success of their activities, but they don't have to be one specific thing. A KPI can be anything that is a relevant and useful measure of your businesses performance – from net or gross profit, website visits or conversions, to social media metrics.

## How do I choose the right KPI?

Your KPIs will depend on many things, such as your industry, the size of your business, or whether it is based on individual or business-wide goals.

**Here are 3 tips for choosing KPIs that work.**

## Make it measurable

To choose the right KPIs, check that what you're using as an indicator of success is measurable, and that it is useful. If you can't measure it, or your measurement isn't useful to your goals, it will only indicate failure – even if you are performing well.

## Hypothesis: Success!

## Keep it simple

Be careful not to select too many KPIs. Choosing just one or two will keep you focussed on achieving your goals.

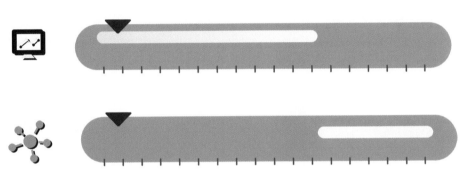

## Review them regularly

Over time, your priorities will change. This means that your KPIs might too. Review your KPIs regularly to ensure that they're relevant to the work you're undertaking at that time, and reflect your overall business goals. A relevant KPI is a useful KPI.

*Chew on this:*
**Do you use KPIs? Are they still relevant to your goals?**

# 16. What's your Big, Hairy, Audacious Goal?

According to Jim Collins and Jerry Porras, your Big, Hairy, Audacious Goal, or BHAG, is a long term goal that will change your entire business. BHAGs are emotionally compelling and encourage strategic planning.

The idea is that people, both within your organisation and outside it, can immediately understand your BHAG and why you want to achieve it.

**Examples of famous BHAGs include:**

- US President JFK's aim to land a man on the moon
- Google's aim to organize the world's information and make it universally accessible and useful
- Sony's aim to change the worldwide perception of Japanese products as poor quality

## How do you choose a Big, Hairy, Audacious Goal?

The first step is to conceptualise it. Ask the question "what goal will change my business forever?" Let your imagination run wild. Imagine a long-term goal (at least 10 years), that is innovative and exciting.

Next, qualify it. Is your goal long term? Is it ambitious, but also realistic? Is it something that not just excites you, but will motivate your team? Will it take your business out of your comfort zone and take it to new planes?

Finally, commit to it. Develop a plan of smaller goals, but maintain focused on how they will help you achieve your BHAG. Use your BHAG to inspire how you run your business on a daily basis.

*Chew on this:*
## What's your BHAG?

# 17. How will you achieve your Big Hairy Audacious Goal?

A Big, Hairy, Audacious Goal (BHAG) should change the nature of your business or industry forever.

Perhaps the famous example is JFK's Moon Challenge, in which he said: "This nation should commit itself to achieving the goal, before this decade is out, of landing a man on the moon and returning him safely to the earth".

A BHAG is meant to **inspire**, but having or trying to set a long term goal of ten or thirty years can be quite daunting for any business owner, no matter how far along your business is.

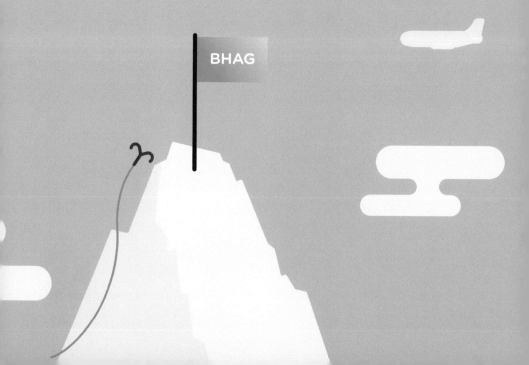

## So how do you make your BHAG more manageable?

**Having a BHAG is pointless unless you plan how you will get there**.
Think of it as climbing a mountain – your BHAG is the summit, and in
order to reach it, not only do you have to be dedicated and passionate
about reaching the top, but you have to plan carefully and aim for
milestones along the way.

Breaking down your goals, and then your actions into weekly, monthly,
and yearly steps will keep you focussed on what you must undertake
to achieve your long-term aims. Just as you might encounter limited
visibility or altitude sickness on the mountain, smaller goals give you the
opportunity to adjust and respond to unexpected obstacles.

There are no straight lines in nature or business – the key to
achieving your BHAG is keeping an eye on the end goal and
adjusting course accordingly.

*Chew on this:*
**How will you implement
the steps to help you
achieve your BHAG?**

51

# Better you, better business

**Personal development tips that
make positive change**

53

# 18. The 3 building blocks of personal branding

Personal branding is what we call the activities you undertake to express to others your value. Rather than marketing your business, it is marketing yourself.

By presenting ourselves in the digital world, we all have a personal brand, whether we intend to or not. Some people are just more aware of how to utilise it and build it into something unique and meaningful.

If you're looking to build your personal brand, here are 3 things it should be based on.

**Your value.** This is a core part of building your personal brand. When looking for connections, partners, or employees, people are really looking for what value someone else can add to their life. Make sure that what you are able to offer others is at the core of your personal brand.

**Your personality & your behaviour.** This is what makes you stand out. Your personality shapes things such as how you approach problems and how you get on with others. Being authentic to yourself and your values is crucial to a good personal brand – if you try to be someone else, others will see through it eventually.

**Your influence.** This is closely tied with both your value and your personality. Your influence is what you can do to make positive change in someone else's life. Whether your influence comes from something quantitative such as good business connections, or you are extremely personable and can motivate a team to do something, you should always play to your strengths when highlighting your ability to influence others.

*Chew on this:*
**How are these three things communicated in your personal brand?**

# 19. Are you a brand or a commodity?

**There are two types of goods and services in the world: commodities and brands.**

Gold, silver, copper, and steel are examples of commodities – you don't pay attention to brand because the gold from one seller is the same as the other. You simply buy from the cheapest vendor. A commodity is a product that serves a function, and does nothing more. A commodity does not add significant value to the customer because it is indistinguishable from the other commodities available.

The value of a brand is harder to calculate, but it can be proven by differentiating from the other commodities within the market.

Humans can be commodities or brands. For example, if your job is to do something entirely functional, your capacity to earn is going to be relatively low. You cannot be differentiated, and can be easily replaced.

Differentiation, therefore, is the best tool a professional can have in an increasingly competitive world. To be irreplaceable, and to create wealth, you must build a brand. The aim is to become the go-to authority in your niche. Think about how you can start marketing yourself so that people trust you above your competitors. Build on this difference and make your personal brand centre around it, making clear that when someone invests in you and your time, that is what they will be getting in return. This way, your customers will choose to work with you because they know the value that you are giving them simply can't be matched by anyone else.

*Chew on this:*

**Why do your customers work with you and not your competitors?**

# 20. Want to be a winner? Develop a winning mindset.

Henry Ford once said

**"whether you think you can or you can't, you're right".**

A winning mindset is a key tool for personal and business growth. It not just helps to define how we think and feel, but what we do and the actions we take.

## So how do you develop a winning mindset?

**Have a purpose**. A business without a real purpose lacks a reason for being and fails to motivate its staff, meaning that it will never grow and develop. The same can be said for individuals. Purpose gives direction to everything we do, and understanding your purpose will help you to understand what you need to do to be going in the right direction.

**Think positive**. There can be a lot of negative external influences in business, from staff difficulties, to costs, to government regulations. Positivity is needed from the top down to overcome these difficulties. Invest time in thinking about the positive elements of your business and communicate them with your team. This will help you to see what you can do, instead of what you can't.

**Have passion**. It's a cliché, but only because it's true. Remember how passionate you were when you started your business, or first led your team? Going into work every day with this passion and excitement will help you create the drive needed to succeed.

*Chew on this:*
**How can you create a winning mindset when things get tough?**

# 21. How to be a winning quitter

'Winners never quit, quitters never win'.

**Or do they?**

We tend to think of quitters as weak – people who can't push themselves to take a challenge. However, that's not strictly true. Some of the time, quitters are actually winners.

## How?

Winning quitters are people who quit something because they know they should. They don't quit because something is too hard, or they're not willing to try, but because the time is right.

Winning quitters know that sometimes, persistence isn't the answer – in fact, it can actually be a sign of someone who doesn't know what to do or how to handle something.

Winning quitters know that reassessing is more effective than persevering with a method that is never going to work.

Winning quitters know that quitting isn't a sign of weakness – it's a sign of strength, belief in yourself, and a willingness to try again.

Winners do quit – just from the right things and at the right times.

*Chew on this:*

**What signs tell you that it's the right time to call it quits?**

# 22. Control what you can

Imagine you want to run the London Marathon. Now imagine that you would like to win. You've trained hard, you're one of the best runners in the country, and you're almost positive that you will end the race with a first place medal.

Now imagine that you lose. **How would that make you feel?**

Despite your assurance that you could win the race, you can't control whether or not you do purely because there are many factors that you don't have the power to control. You may suffer an injury or illness, the course may not suit your running style, you just may not function at 100% capacity on the day, or there simply may be better runners than you taking part.

But whilst you cannot control the outcome, there are many things that you can control, such as making sure that you have prepared and trained, eating well and staying hydrated, and investing in the best running equipment.

Whether it's in your personal or professional life, it can be difficult when something doesn't go your way. Companies – and individuals – can waste huge amounts of emotional and physical capital by failing to focus on the things they can control, rather than the things they can't.

When things go wrong in business, it can be easy to blame the market, the economy, or your competitors, but none of these things are productive. Instead, it's wise – and more productive – to adjust your attitude and your approach, just as you may adjust your effort levels in a difficult race.

Make your focus the things that you can control and see where it gets you. I guarantee that it will be further than if you focus on the things that you can't.

*Chew on this:*
**How do you approach a challenge? What things do you try and take control of to maximise your chances of success?**

# 23. Mastering time management

As the saying goes, there aren't enough hours in the day. Everybody has the same amount of hours, so how do some people make time work for them? Here are 4 tips.

## Don't be instantly available

Answering your emails and phone calls when they come in, no matter what you're doing, might make you feel like you're being efficient, but those few minutes here and there add up. Prioritising communication is a great way to save on time. Check your emails in the morning and then again in the afternoon to minimise distractions, and don't answer the phone if you're too busy.

## Don't multitask

Multitasking is great... until it isn't. Sometimes we try to achieve so much that we actually achieve very little. Try blocking out chunks of time during the week where you focus on one thing, and one thing only.

## Keep meetings focused

We all hate long meetings, especially when we have something else to be doing. Keep them short by setting agendas and curbing any discussion that goes off topic. You should also try blocking all your meetings together, leaving you the rest of the day or week to finish work.

## Delegate

It can be tempting to take on a big project yourself rather than spend precious time explaining the details of it to someone else. However, the time taken to delegate tasks appropriately can save you more time in the long run than quickly finishing it off yourself. This will give you the time to get on with vital work, as well as the peace of mind that your employees are busy being productive.

*Chew on this:*
**What tasks take up most of your time? Are they necessary, or can they be delegated?**

# 24. It's smart to be the dumbest person in the room

You might have heard the saying, "if you're the smartest person in the room, you're in the wrong room".

In surrounding yourself with smarter or more experienced people, you will collectively generate more ideas, more discussion, and more solutions. You can learn from other people's input, and constantly be learning from those around you. On the other hand, if you are the smartest person in the room, it's practically impossible to develop – after all, you can't just learn from yourself.

## But what about appearing to be the dumbest person in the room?

Here's why it's actually a smart move.

Being the 'dumbest' person in the room can actually help to create a more solid understanding of what you need to do, as well as help influence effective communication. Next time you're discussing a specific project or process, try asking simple questions such as

- **How does this work?**
- **How long will it take?**
- **Is this necessary?**

Appearing to ask 'dumb' questions is not a pointless exercise. In doing so, you will ensure that you cover every small detail. This means you're more likely to avoid realising that you have overlooked an essential element before you're mid-project and it's too late to go back and correct it.

> *Chew on this:*
> **Have you been the smartest person in the room before? Did you learn much?**

# 25. The importance of peer groups

You might have heard the phrase, "If you're green you grow, if you're ripe you rot."

**But what does it mean?**

In business, learning is always a priority. You can never know enough. If you stop learning, you will start to fail.

Every one of us has three key groups in our professional lives that are a steady source of learning. These are...

Optimism
Boldness
Risk Taking
Rule breaker

**Those ahead of you**. These people set the benchmarks and goals you should strive to achieve. Learn from them and one day, you will be a role model for someone in your current position.

**Those on our peer level.** We can learn from our peers through sharing our experiences. Supporting each other in our journeys means that we are constantly working together to seek solutions for the challenges we face on a daily basis.

**Those behind you in their journey.** These people give us the opportunity to learn through mentoring. Showing others the path is a good way to reflect on what you already know and on what other paths you could have taken. Remember – when one teaches, two learn. That's why they say 'the best way to learn is to teach'.

*Chew on this:*
**What is the most valuable lessons you have learnt during your career, and how does it influence you today?**

# Mastering decision making

Everything you need to know to
make up your mind

# 26. Beware the perils of confirmation bias

Nazir wants to buy a new top of the range Range Rover. His reasons why were...

**"It would enable me to carry lots of equipment!"**

*Actually, in the past two years he has never had to carry anything larger than a briefcase or set of golf clubs.*

**"It would help me beat the traffic and get to work in the worst ice and snow!"**

*Actually, the last time winter weather seriously disrupted road travel for more than a couple of days was in 1963.*

**"I will be able to travel in comfort and visit clients all over the country!"**

*Actually, all of Nazir's clients are all based within 50 miles of his office.*

EN

LC

Nazir went ahead and bought his Range Rover that sat for a year as a wonderful but useless piece of jewellery on his drive. Paying for the Range Rover eventually bankrupted his business and it had to be returned to the leasing company.

Confirmation bias is the opposite of evidence-based decision making. It's based upon deciding to do something and then constructing the evidence to justify your decision. Often, decision making is emotional – Nazir really wanted his Range Rover as a status symbol, but constructed reasons to make his decision more logical.

It's important to honestly consider why we make our decisions. Make big decisions in a considered way, test the decision, and critique it as far as you can with a critical friend. Ultimately, the evidence will show you the way - if your decision doesn't stack up, it isn't worth making.

IONAL

CAL

*Chew on this:*
**How do you usually make big decisions? Do you let your emotions get in the way?**

# 27. The solution to your problem may be counter intuitive

The mother of a young family got into conversation with a leading safety expert. She was concerned about keeping her young children safe around water, and expected the expert to recommend a good swimming teacher.

His advice, however, took her by surprise.

> **"If you want to make sure that your children do not drown, make sure they never learn to swim."**

Crazy advice? Perhaps not. Statistics show that the people most at risk of drowning are those who consider themselves strong swimmers, as they're more likely to get themselves into trouble by overestimating their ability. On the other hand, people who cannot swim are afraid of water and tend to keep away from it.

## The moral of the story?

In looking for answers, beware of the blindingly obvious. Take time to reflect on all your options and gather opinions from all sources – even junior staff or people that you may regard as irrelevant. The best solution may be just what you would never have expected.

*Chew on this:*

**Think of a big decision you must make soon. Who can you get involved that might offer a fresh perspective?**

75

# 28. Work the problem

In April 1970, Apollo 13 was preparing for its third flight to land men on the moon.

Unfortunately, it ran into serious trouble on the journey when the main spacecraft suffered what was later shown to be an explosion in an oxygen tank due to an electrical fault. Over the coming days there were many occasions when it looked a serious possibility that the three astronauts aboard would be lost in space forever.

On hearing that there was a major incident, the flight controller, Gene Kranz, reportedly got his team together quickly with words which have now become world famous:

> **"Let's work the problem, people. Let's not make things worse by guessing."**

Despite the immense pressure and the need to act quickly, the remarkable skill, steadiness, and smart improvisation by the astronauts and ground crew, led by Kranz, managed to return the men safely to earth.

Too often in stressful situations, we act on impulse and end up making a bad situation worse. Although we will probably never know the pressure of leading someone back to the safety of Earth, it's important to remember Kranz's example when we feel under pressure.

The most difficult thing in these situations is to keep a calm head, but it is also the most important. Remember to use all the information available to you in order to reach a considered judgement - and consider yourself lucky that you're not landing a rocket!

*Chew on this:*
**How does pressure affect your ability to make decisions, and what can you do about it?**

# 29. Do you have a fixed or open mindset?

**Do you have everything figured out?**

**Do you know exactly how to do X, and Y, and Z?**

**Are you an expert at these things?**

**Do you always do everything in the same, precise way?**

In other words, do you have a fixed mindset?

When you are set in your way of thinking, it can be hard to see the alternatives. Especially if your way works.

A person with an open mindset, on the other hand, is always looking for alternatives. Not because their way doesn't work, but because they know that their way could always be improved. They are always looking to learn, grow and find new ways of doing things better.

Having an open mindset is how you truly become an expert – not by doing everything 'right' every time, but by being willing to try and find a new approach that improves on your last one. A fixed mindset, on the other hand, will make you complacent, eventually leaving you in the dust. An open mindset will make you a master, and someone who is always ready for the next challenge.

*Chew on this:*
**Could you be more open to new ideas and solutions?**

79

# 30. Because we can, does not mean we should

Top neurosurgeon Henry Marsh has some wonderful stories and advice in his excellent book about his life and career in brain surgery, 'Do No Harm'. Perhaps surprisingly, much of what he says can be applied to business.

Perhaps one of the most telling comments from Marsh is,

**"knowing not to operate is just as important as knowing how to operate, and is much more difficult to acquire."**

As you may well know, the battle cry of the boardroom is usually **'something must be done!'**

## But must something always be done?

Looking back on a distinguished career, Henry Marsh says that some of his biggest regrets have been inappropriate operations that, whilst technically feasible, have left a patient no better or worse than when they went into theatre.

It seems counterintuitive to the entrepreneurial temperament, but sometimes in business - as in the operating theatre - the 'do nothing' option really is the best option. It's just knowing when to use it.

81

# Some lessons in leadership

It all starts and ends with leadership

1

2

3

# 31. Sir Alex Ferguson on leadership and the importance of respect

Sir Alex Ferguson is one of the most successful football club managers of all time. During his career as Manager of Manchester United, he won 49 trophies and turned the club in to a leading global brand.

Sir Alex knows his football, but what can we as business leaders learn from his success? It all comes down to his view on gaining respect.

He has been quoted as saying,

**"You don't get the best out of people by hitting them with an iron rod. You do so by gaining their respect, getting them accustomed to triumphs and convincing them that they are capable of improving their performance."**

As a leader you don't need to be loved.

Being liked - or even loved - is nice, but it's not necessary for respect. However, ruling by fear is not the right way either – your team might do what you want if they fear you, but they will never do it well or for the right reasons.

Above all, a leader needs to be respected. This is the key to effective leadership. How you achieve respect will depend on your team, and your organisation. Listen to others, pick up on the signals that they respond to, and use this to influence your leadership style.

**Respect is the universal quality of successful leadership.**

Earn it.

*Chew on this:*
**Why is respect important to you?**

# 32. Leading from the back

**What does it mean to be a great leader?**

- To be strong?
- To be confident?
- To have authority?

These are all important things, but they are not what makes a great leader. Being a leader is not about yourself, or your qualities – it's about putting your team first.

In short, a great leader knows how to 'lead from the back'.

When you lead a team, you should support them to reach their ambitions and goals, as this will help you to achieve yours. Fostering a talented team and watching them succeed should inspire your drive to succeed

– not just the other way round. Leadership is not about producing followers, but producing future leaders.

So how can you do this?

You could ask your team questions, encourage them to lead a project outside of their comfort zone, or foster an environment where employees can freely express their opinions.

Learn to lead from the back, and cultivate a team that can truly flourish on their own. After all, you can't progress without them.

*Chew on this:*
**What does being a leader mean to you?**

# 33. Why CEOs should overcome the social struggle

Social media, with its ever changing nature, can easily be seen as a vast unknown – something that can't be automated or properly measured. That is, at least not before it changes again.

According to Thomas Power, social marketing expert, most CEOs are reluctant to engage with social media. He says that they either don't see the value in social media, or don't have the skills to use it. But there are good reasons why C-Level execs should embrace social media. Here are just three of them.

**To build brand trust**
As a CEO, being involved in social social media can help humanise your brand. Seeing a high level employee engaging with others online will increase transparency and give your audience faith that your business will face their customer concerns head on.

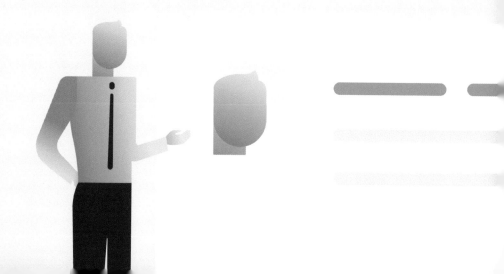

**To increase your network**

When you think about it, it's the people behind the brand that really interests others – that's why Richard Branson and Mark Zuckerberg are people of significant interest. Having the CEO on social media adds another element to your audience's engagement with a brand.

**To be a thought leader**

Being a CEO online offers a wealth of different opportunities for engagement with your audience. By being on social media, you can offer your audience more than just tweets about your product – being a CEO online means you can share your knowledge, expertise, and industry insights. This will encourage a perception of your brand as an industry leader.

*Chew on this:*
**Are you on social media? Why, and what benefits does it afford your business? Can you harness these further?**

# Building a winning team

## How to hire and inspire a team that gets results

# 34. How to hire the best candidate for the job

You might think that recruiting the best candidate to fill a position in your business is all about choosing the person with the best qualifications and experience.

But what if I were to tell you that the best person for the job isn't always the person with the most experience?

This is the idea behind *strengths-based recruitment*.

Whereas traditional competency interviews assess whether a person can **do** the job, strengths-based recruitment assesses whether the person will **enjoy** the job. Instead of asking for examples of experience, strengths-based recruitment is designed to find out about a candidate's strengths and interests.

Questions might include things such as:

- Describe your most successful day
- What is more important – the small details or the bigger picture?
- What subject did you enjoy most at school and why?
- What is the one thing on your to-do-list that you always leave until last?

Using strengths-based recruitment means you are more likely to hire the candidate who will enjoy their work, and therefore be more likely to be motivated to succeed. Because of this, they are also more likely to stay with your business for longer.

*Chew on this:*
**How can using strengths-based recruitment help you find the best fit for your team?**

# 35. The secret to building great teams

Take a moment to consider this story...

In the early 1960's, during a trip to NASA, President John Kennedy met with staff ranging from astronauts, engineers, flight controllers, and other support workers. During the trip, he was taken to the staff canteen and met a woman who was clearing plates and wipingdown tables.

Perhaps rather foolishly, the President asked the woman

**"And what do you do?"**

The woman replied, **"I am helping to put a man on the moon."**

Great teams aren't just made of typically "great" people. Great teams bring together people with different jobs and skills. More importantly, however, great teams have a shared belief in what they are working to achieve.

The woman in the story may have just been wiping tables, but she was an essential part of an organisation that was working towards great things. She had been convinced of, and truly believed in, the **"why"**, demonstrating the true power of a team in which everyone understands the goal they are working towards and are in an environment in which they all feel valued.

*Chew on this:*

**What can you do to make your team feel great?**

# 36. How to spot potential leaders in your business

Imagine that your most senior manager just stepped down from their role unexpectedly. **Would your business be equipped to plug the gap in leadership?**

Here are three tips for identifying which of your employees is a potential leader.

## Potential, not performance

Ability is important in a leader, but it isn't everything. Just because someone is good at what they do, it doesn't mean they're able to show others how to do it. Look beyond employee performance, and consider their willingness to learn and take on new tasks. A leader should always be looking to learn before they lead.

## Do they make things happen?

Some people are content to watch from the side-lines, or do as they're told. Future leaders, on the other hand, will engage in discussion and take action when there's a decision to be made. If there's someone in your business who always takes initiative to say or do something, they're probably made of leadership material.

## Look for personal development

The best way to spot potential leaders is to give them the tools to become one. Training and development will help you not just identify who has a natural potential for leadership, but who can develop that natural edge into a significant characteristic. As a business leader, investing in formal training will give you a team who are ready to take the leap into any position that is required of them.

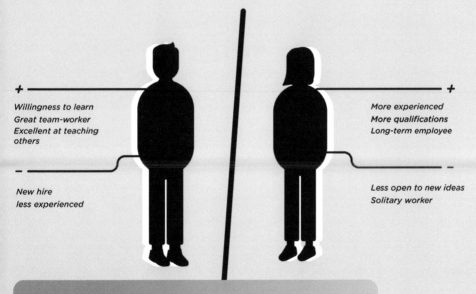

+ ———————————————————

*Willingness to learn*
*Great team-worker*
*Excellent at teaching others*

– ———————————————————

*New hire*
*less experienced*

+ ———————————————————

*More experienced*
*More qualifications*
*Long-term employee*

– ———————————————————

*Less open to new ideas*
*Solitary worker*

*Chew on this:*
### How have you identified leaders in the past? How well did it work?

97

# 37. The exception to the rule

In a quarter of a century, Sir Alex Ferguson had a telephone directory of great players under his management, including four who were, in his view, world class - Paul Scholes, Ryan Giggs, Eric Cantona and Christiano Ronaldo.

Sir Alex was known for not accepting anything less than the best from his players, occasionally losing his temper when they did not perform as expected. However, the story goes that Sir Alex had a soft spot for Cantona, letting him get away with many things that other players would not.

This goes against the golden rule of managing people: be consistent, even-handed, and careful not to show favouritism - few things inspire discord more quickly than a feeling that some people are being treated differently to others.

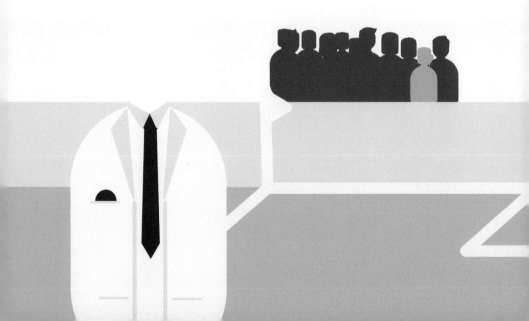

## But is it okay to have an exception to the rule?

A manager who is fair and makes the same demands upon all employees is likely to be respected. However, as any manager knows, it can be hard to be firm in the case of some employees.

Often mavericks, these employees are usually very talented, but find it difficult to adhere to strict rules and regulations. In fact, they perform best when unrestricted and left to their own devices. You are more likely to earn respect from these people if you let them show you what they are capable of, and don't stop them from doing things their own way. In this case, there is an exception to the rule – but you must be sure of the reasons for doing this. An exception to the rule must return exceptional results.

*Chew on this:*
**How do you manage 'exceptions to the rule' employees and how does it affect their performance?**

# 38. Match the temperament to the role

**What do you look for when hiring a candidate for a job? The right qualifications? Extensive experience?**

One of the key factors in selecting the right person for any job is getting the individual with the right temperament.

**But what constitutes the 'right' temperament?**

As an **entrepreneur** looking to inspire a team or explore business development opportunities, you might look for **courage, optimism, boldness, willingness to take a risk, not always playing by the book, and an inclination to try something different.**

But do we want these qualities in a **pilot**, or a **dentist**? At the controls of an aircraft, or with a scalpel in hand, courage to try something new becomes corner-cutting and willingness to take a risk becomes risky behaviour.

**Pilots need to be methodical, cautious, and risk averse** – all those things that probably will not sit high on the person specification of an entrepreneur.

It's essential to recognise that for different roles, we not only need people with differing skills and experience, but also with a temperament appropriate to the job.

*Chew on this:*

**Which has been more useful to you in your career - your experience, or your temperament?**

101

# 39. Coaching and mentoring

For many people, the difference between coaching and mentoring isn't clear. In business, we tend to separate the two words, although sometimes they do get used interchangeably. There are, however, distinct differences. Here is a quick guide to the difference between the two.

## What is coaching?

Coaching is aimed at helping to develop skills in a particular area, and is usually short-term and task oriented. Coaching is driven by a need to acquire skills and knowledge and improve a return on investment (ROI) for the individual.

Coach     **TEACHER**     Mentor

## What is mentoring?

Mentoring is more long-term and is built on a relationship. It's about working to achieve an overall transformation, rather than working to develop one particular area. The aim is not the achievement of goals but the successful management of them. As the aim is not to overcome one particular challenge, it can be harder to measure.

## But is it possible for both coaching and mentoring to exist side by side?

Consider, *for example*, the role of a teacher. They provide both coaching and mentoring by giving short-term support to overcome a task, such as improving a test result, as well as offering also a long-term support in trying to transform or maintain students' behaviour and achievements. A good teacher is capable of both these things alongside each other - just as a good business person is. The key is understanding the role of each relationship and how they support one another. When it comes to building a winning team, long-term relationships - such as those which are built through mentoring - can extremely beneficial when it comes to effectively encouraging and coaching individuals in overcoming a particular difficulty.

*Chew on this:*
**Do you use coaching, mentoring, or a mixture of both?**

103

# Growing your business

Top tips for communicating your value and delivering results

# 40. What makes a brand?

Your brand is probably the most valuable asset your business or organisation has. However, too many people fail to understand what brand is and what it is not.

Many people think that a brand is a clever and readily recognised logo, such as Coca-Cola or Google's famous and familiar logos.

This is wrong. Brand is much more. Brand is intangible. Yes, brand is about the look and feel of a business, but it is also - more importantly - about your values and behaviours.

Take BMW, for example.

BMW's strong brand image is based around building cars with cutting-edge engineering that lives up to the business's claim to provide 'the ultimate driving machine'. BMW is not a successful brand simply because their cars have a nice badge.

Brand **has to be** about something more than a logo because if it wasn't, the reputation of big companies could be destroyed far more easily. Take Toyota and Volkswagen, for example. Both have seen their fair share of scandal - whether about build quality or emissions scams. However, both companies have survived and successfully recovered because they have strong and trusted brands, established over many years.

A strong brand will be forgiven its mistakes provided errors are admitted and clear steps are taken to put matters right. Relying on a new logo to make right any mistakes is never going to work.

*Chew on this:*
**How do you define your brand beyond your look?**

107

# 41. How to walk the talk

Many businesses and organisations are all too keen to paper their walls with a fancy vision and long mission statement. All too often, however, these mission statements are not worth the paper on which they are written.

Having a vision or mission statement for your business is all well and good, but unless it encapsulates a set of values and behaviours that are *actually lived out* in the day-to-day running of your business, you will inevitably find that there is a divide between what your business sets out to achieve and what it actually achieves.

So how can you make sure that your business's mission statement is meaningful? The key is clarity. Too many mission statements are full of fluff and fine words. To be effective, every person at every level of your business should understand what your mission statement means and what is expected of them in order to fulfil it.

Ryanair's slogan, for example, is "Low fares. Made simple." In their marketing, there is a clear statement that the passenger will not get a cheaper flight elsewhere. This is a proposition that is easily understood and consistently delivered. In the last three decades, Ryanair has grown into one of the busiest international airlines due to its straightforward approach to delivery and representation of its service.

In essence, Ryanair says what it does and does what it says.

As they say, actions speak louder than words. If you must use words, make sure your actions align.

*Chew on this:*

**How do you live up to your mission statement in your daily activities?**

# 42. Train to make a good first impression

The old adage 'first impressions last longest' may feel unfair, but the fact is that it's very true. Bad first impressions can be hard to put right, and in business, there's a lot of places where you're making those impressions.

One of the common mistakes SMEs make is to underrate the importance of the receptionist, for example. As these businesses have less resource and stretched managers, they often delegate these tasks to junior members of staff, such as an apprentice. A potentially even bigger mistake is to pass social media and marketing to a junior member of the team with little supervision and guidance.

Consider apprenticeships. They are a fantastic and cost-effective way of both gaining resource and training that resource to be experts in your area. However, in small businesses, apprentices will likely have more responsibility – including responsibility for the impression your business makes on customers and stakeholders.

Training, therefore is vital – not just for apprentices, but for all staff – on how what they do impacts your business's reputation. A mentor who understands the area of expertise can pass on their knowledge and help develop your staff member to the point where they can be trusted to make a good first impression in everything they do.

Your first impression could be the difference between winning and losing clients, or more importantly, your reputation. You should invest in getting it right.

*Chew on this:*
**How do you ensure your staff make a good impression?**

# 43. Be heard above the noise

**Ideas have always entered society through communication.**

Hundreds of years ago, when the printing press was a new technology, producing a book was an expensive activity. Since then, the introduction of new communication technologies has seen the emergence of more ways to produce and share knowledge. This has created a wider economy of knowledge sharing. While this is incredibly useful for users, it can be harder for businesses and producers of knowledge to get their ideas heard.

So how can your business be heard above the noise? It comes down to two things.

**Be the best.** The first way to win in the knowledge economy is to become the best in your niche or industry. In order to do this, you have to keep track of what's going on – the latest thoughts, ideas, and trends.

**Bring value.** You don't have to monetise knowledge. Many share what they know for free. It might seem strange to give away your knowledge for free, but in a world where people are always searching for information, giving away your ideas is not only a great way to find business, but to bring value to your audience so that next time they will remember you.

Be the best at what you do. Bring value to the world. It's that simple.

*Chew on this:*

**How do you get your business heard above everyone else?**

113

# 44. The importance of respecting your competition

It's easy to look down on your competition or even claim that no-one can compete with you, but you can learn a lot from respecting your competitors and remembering that we have a lot in common.

Here are 3 ways you can learn from our competition.

## Identifying and improving on their weaknesses

By understanding your competitor's strengths, you can also focus on their weaknesses and ask ourselves *what can I learn from this*? Make their weaknesses your strengths to truly differentiate your business.

## Taking inspiration from their successes

Where your competitors are doing well, ask yourself *how can I do this better, or differently?* Factors such as personalised services or competitive prices are simple ways of improving the services that you offer.

## Joining forces

Unconventional, but incredibly powerful. By considering a strategic alliance, you will be able to draw on both of your strengths and help each other improve your weaknesses.

Nothing teaches you better than your competition – we need them to constantly drive us forward. When you fear competition, what you really fear is your own shortcomings. Respect your competition, but more importantly – learn from them.

> *Chew on this:*
> **What can you learn from your competitors?**

# 45. Shovels or teaspoons?

Picture this.

Someone asks you to dig a giant hole in the ground, and offers you a shovel and a teaspoon.

## Which do you pick?

The correct answer depends on how you are getting paid. If you are in a job where you make an hourly wage, you should pick the teaspoon. Why? Because the longer you can make the task last, the more money you make. It might not be the most efficient way of digging the hole, but someone is prepared to pay you for the hours it takes to get the job done.

If you are an entrepreneur, however, chances are you are getting paid by the number of holes you dig. It doesn't matter *how fast you dig*, but rather *how many holes you dig and how well you do it*.

Elon Musk, CEO of SpaceX and Tesla, recently announced that he is working on a 3D boring machine to dig giant underground tunnels – because he was sick of Los Angeles traffic. Initially, people didn't take Musk seriously, but news reports suggest that he has already tested a 30ft wide, 50ft long, and 15ft deep trench at SpaceX's headquarters. It might sound crazy now, but Musk's venture is clearly aimed at disrupting current norms and creating a new innovative way in which the world works.

In business, you're hardly ever celebrated for the time you put in. No one's client has ever said "What a great project - it took you over 500 hours to get done!". As a business owner, the world rewards you for the **value you create**, or how many good quality holes you can dig, not the time you spent to create that value.

As such, you should choose your tools wisely. Remember to always ask yourself "what tools are going to help me create the best value for this client?"

*Chew on this:*
**How do you create value for your customers?**

# 46. Dear client, you're sacked

As any business owner knows, **it costs a lot more to win a new client than to keep an existing one**. That's why it's important to look after the business we already have by going the extra mile and treating them well.

But all businesses will have bad clients – perhaps they're bad at paying bills, or are unappreciative and make unreasonable demands. They might have employed you for your expert knowledge, but will constantly challenge what you do and act as if they know your job better than you do.

**The difficulty of a client is in inverse proportion to the value of the work**, and often you can end up giving disproportionate time and effort to an unappreciative client who might not even pay you on time.

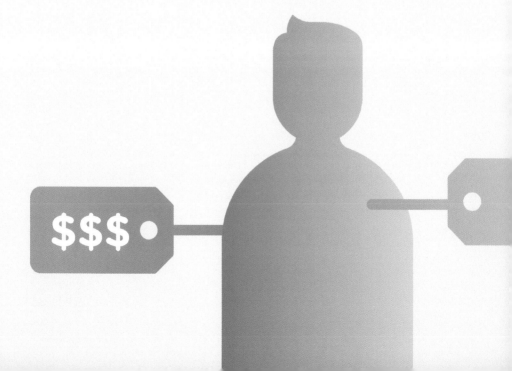

So what should you do? Clients are, of course, entitled to ask questions and make certain demands.

The key is to recognise the point at which they cross the line and hinder your ability to provide them with a good service.

Look into your heart and mind and ask if you are doing a good job or if your client has just cause to be unhappy. If this is the case, recognise the need to address the issue. However, if you are trying hard to do what is best for your client, evaluate whether you need their custom. Bad clients are a drain and they undermine confidence. Sometimes, as difficult and counterintuitive as it may seem, it can be best to say 'thanks but no thanks.'

*Chew on this:*
**How can you deal with difficult clients better?**

# 47. A lesson in entrepreneurship from the Chinese bamboo tree

## Do you know how the Chinese bamboo tree grows?

Once it first sprouts, it takes six weeks for the Chinese bamboo tree to grow to the size of a 9 storey building. But it does not take just six weeks for the Chinese bamboo tree to grow – it actually takes five years.

Once planted, the ground around the Chinese bamboo tree has to be watered and fertilized for five years before the tree even breaks the surface of the earth. That means, for each Chinese bamboo tree you see, a farmer spent five years watering and nurturing the ground.

## But what has this got to do with entrepreneurship?

Often when we look at other people's businesses, what we see is simply their success – not the time spent trying to achieve it. In other words, we see their six weeks of growth, not the five years spent nurturing their business to get it to that point. You must remember not to feel deterred if your business isn't growing as quickly as you hoped. Remember, it takes time and dedication to grow a business. It takes time to build the foundation, and to get the right people. It takes time to build up a network, and to learn the market. It takes time to figure it out.

If your tree hasn't blossomed yet, have faith, have patience, and keep going with consistent action until it does.

*Chew on this:*

**What actions do you take that are successful in achieving growth, and how can you build on these?**

# 48. To stand still is to go backwards

To stand still is to go backwards.

What does this mean?

Sir David Brailsford is one of the most successful and dedicated people in the world of cycling. He is acclaimed for his work both with the Great Britain Cycling team and Team Sky.

Sir David holds a simple view that helps him achieve his success, drawn from the physics of riding a bike. He goes by the fact that *if you stop going forward, you will fall off.* Anyone who has ever ridden a bicycle will be familiar with the principle

The same principle can be applied to business. It will not always be possible to make giant strides, but it is always possible to take small

steps and continue going forward. Sir David calls this 'marginal gains' and it has been at the core to driving success in all the organisations where he has worked.

In the cycling world, this could be making marginal improvements to clothing or making sure that sleeping arrangements for top riders ensure that they will be properly rested. In business, it could be streamlining your processes, or updating your website. These things don't seem like huge leaps, and probably won't give you the same satisfaction as winning a big client, but each improvement you make is a small step towards growth and success.

Keep moving forward, even if you can only manage small steps, and understand the importance of marginal gains.

*Chew on this:*
**How do you keep your business moving forward at all times?**

# Innovation and technology

**Keeping your business
up to date**

# INBOX

| | | | |
|---|---|---|---|
| **Check this TEDx Talk out** | | | |
| **Collaboration opportunity?** | | | |
| **Looking for advice on...** | 23:59 | 22/09/17 | Bal Powers |
| **Good article on Networking** | 8:01 | 22/09/17 | Jane Jameson |
| **New Canny Bites video** | 03:27 | 20/09/17 | Saf Ali |
| **re: campaign costs** | 17.28 | 20/09/17 | Rich Gold |

# 49. Digitalisation: business on demand

You might have heard of digitisation, which is the process of turning analogue information into digital information, but have you heard of digitalisation?

Digitalisation is the ongoing action of sharing knowledge in a digital format. Businesses are increasingly turning to the internet to share their insights through digital content, including videos, infographics, and podcasts.

## Why is this?

We live in an 'on-demand world'. Our television is on-demand, our shopping is on-demand, and we can communicate with friends online, on-demand. The internet allows us more control and freedom over how we live our lives. Your business should also be 'on-demand' in order to keep your audience engaged.

## So how can you do this?

Digitalisation is about sharing knowledge. Creating digital content that adds value to your customer where needed means that they can engage with your business as and when they want.

A video demonstrating how to use your product can be watched at your customer's convenience at whatever moment they are handling your product. A podcast discussing relevant news to your industry can be listened to at any time, in any place, whenever your audience feels the need to learn more.

In other words, digitalisation lets your audience find your business in the moment they need to, rather than you coming to them, hoping that they need your services.

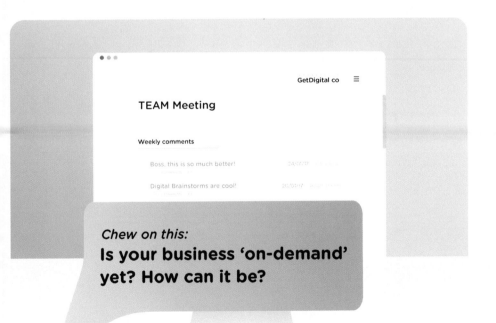

*Chew on this:*
**Is your business 'on-demand' yet? How can it be?**

# 50. Digitalisation: a how to guide

Digitisation allows your audience to engage with your business on their terms – when and where they need you. Understanding the importance of needing to digitalise is one thing, but how can we begin to become a business 'on-demand'?

There are many ways that your business can approach digitalisation. Here are just a few ideas.

## Video

Video is the fastest growing digital sector. More people are turning to the internet for information, and video is the quickest way of getting a message across. As business leaders, creating a content-driven business strategy will add value to your customers. Consider using video to showcase how your product works or to provide valuable information about what your audience needs to know about your industry. Treat this not as a sales opportunity, but as a chance to give something valuable to your customers.

## Infographics

Much like video, infographics are a great way of communicating information. Making creative and engaging infographics is an easy way of making data more appealing to your audience. Infographics can also easily be shared on social media, meaning your audience can engage with your business in spaces that aren't sales-orientated.

## Powerpoints

Powerpoints aren't typically considered as a form of content that can help engage your audience, as they're often used internally rather than externally. However, there's a certain power in using them to share knowledge – audiences can view content slide by slide, as and when they please. SlideShare, by LinkedIn, is a useful tool used by top brands like Samsung and IBM for hosting presentations.

*Chew on this:*
**Does your business use any of these methods? If not, is it time to?**

129

# 51. Moving up the innovation curve: the risks and rewards of innovation

If you have ever studied marketing, you might have seen the innovation curve. In essence, any innovation usually goes through five stages:

- Innovators
- Early adopters
- Early majority
- Late majority
- Laggards

Innovators buy and use new products as soon as they come out. They keep up to date with the latest innovations, and pre-order or wait in line for the newest technology, and generally stay "ahead of the curve".

In business, it used to be the case that being in the middle, or even towards the end, of the curve was fine - just as long as you weren't a laggard and managed to get better prices, information, and feedback on the technology. The innovators were seen as the risk takers, who invested in new tools before they were tried and tested.

These days, however, there is an increased risk of not being an innovator. In the digital age, everyone is able to keep up to date on next best thing. Failing to keep up to date with the latest technology means you are more likely to lose competitive advantage, especially as technology is growing and adapting at an increasing rate. Wait too long to adopt a new tool, and it may be out of date by the time the cash leaves your account.

In order to stay ahead of the curve, remember that the time to act is always now.

*Chew on this:*
**Have you ever been in the first wave to adopt a new technology? How about the last? How did this affect your business differently?**

# 52. Grassroots innovation

Leaders are often thought as innovators – the brains behind the business, and consequently, behind the success.

However, innovation inspired from the grassroots is a growing trend in business. Harnessing the innovative power of your workforce is a great way to affect real change, because the ideas come from those who manage the day-to-day handling of your business.

A bottom-up approach not only means you have a wider pool of ideas, but also that your employees are empowered to take control of those aspects of your business that need improving. This can inspire an overhaul of company culture, and even help your business to push past any plateaus in growth.

So, how can you influence grassroots innovation in your business?

**Collaboration is key.** Include different people in problem-solving sessions, or encourage regular open discussions around the workplace. This will foster an environment where employees can confidently put forward their ideas.

**Create a community for ideas**. Consider developing a platform, such as an intranet or forum, for employees to to freely and democratically share ideas.

**Promote a system of continuous feedback.** This will allow for an ongoing discourse where innovative ideas can be developed.

*Chew on this:*
**How could the ideas and opinions of your employees change your business for the better?**

# About the author

Safaraz Ali began his career in the financial services sector and since 1999, has been involved in the world of business in one way or another. He is the Head of Pathway Group, a workforce development solutions provider, specialising in apprenticeship training and recruitment.

Safaraz created Pathway2Grow, which has the tag line "Network, Learn, and Grow", with the vision to conduct business networking differently through creating a vibrant network that develops and serves business communities nationally.

Through the vehicle of TCI Pathway Ltd, Safaraz offers Independent strategy, advice, and investment for private businesses specialising in social care, education, training, and recruitment sectors. It offers support and guidance in developing and executing growth strategies, raising funds for growth strategies, and managing growth.

**You can contact Safaraz on his social media feeds:**
https://uk.linkedin.com/in/safaraz
www.twitter.com/SafarazAli
www.youtube.com/user/safaraz

25695888R00081

Printed in Poland
by Amazon Fulfillment
Poland Sp. z o.o., Wrocław